ASTRAL WEEKS, ETC.

poems by

Brookes Moody

Finishing Line Press
Georgetown, Kentucky

ASTRAL WEEKS, ETC.

for Dad and for Mom
for always having music playing

Copyright © 2025 by **Brookes Moody**
ISBN 979-8-88838-870-9 First Edition
All rights reserved under International and Pan-American Copyright Conventions. No part of this book may be reproduced in any manner whatsoever without written permission from the publisher, except in the case of brief quotations embodied in critical articles and reviews.

Publisher: Leah Huete de Maines
Editor: Christen Kincaid
Cover Art: Louise Lennon, "The Old Lane"
Author Photo: Erin McGinn
Cover Design: Brookes Moody

Order online: www.finishinglinepress.com
also available on amazon.com

Author inquiries and mail orders:
Finishing Line Press
PO Box 1626
Georgetown, Kentucky 40324
USA

Contents

Liner Notes 1

I. If I Ventured in the Slipstream

The First Draft of *Astral Weeks*, or The Emotional Labor of
    Janet "Planet" Rigsbee Morrison 4
At the Langhorne Slim Show, East Side Milwaukee 5
Between the Viaducts of Your Dreams—for Alyssa 6
folklore 7
Beside You 8
I Shall Watch the Ferryboats and They'll Get High 9
For Bob, at Ben's Wedding 10
Sam Cooke is on the Radio and the Night is Filled With Space 11
Fret Noise 12
Between the Viaducts of Your Dreams—for Dad 13
And It Stoned Me, Prelude 14
It Stoned Me Just Like Going Home 15
Caught One More Time Up on Cyprus Avenue 17
Dweller on the Threshold 18
The Last Time I was Drunk 19
The Sweet Inspirations, or in Defense of "Brown Eyed Girl" 20
While Walking Routinely to and From Work 21
Dwelling 23
Warren Zevon Poems 25
Meditating to Madame George 26
On Probably Not Being Pharrell 27

II. Turn Up Your Radio

Greenwich Mean Time 30
Bill Remembers Watkins Glen 31
Wendy Remembers Watkins Glen 32
Stuart Remembers Van Morrison and Janis Joplin at the Cole
    Auditorium, University of Maryland, Friday, June 19, 1970 33
Annotated Listening: "Live at the Grand Opera House Belfast" 34

    From Forest Hills Stadium, September 12, 2018 37
    What *Pet Sounds* Means to Me, or Franklin and I Go See
        Brian Wilson.. 38

III. Old Old Woodstock

    Dominique in Woodstock, NY, 1967.. 40
    Imagining West Saugerties... 41
    4% Pantomime 42
    Van at *The Last Waltz* 43
    Morrison and Dylan Perform "Foreign Window"................................. 44

IV. Looking for the Veedon Fleece

    A Mischief of Two... 46
    Looking for the Veedon Fleece... 47
    The Streets of Arklow 49
    Box of Rain.. 51
    Purple Heather 52
    Northern Ireland Poetry 53
    Queens of the Slipstream 55
    Ways of Looking at "Foreign Window" 56

V. Still for Searching for the Philosopher's Stone

    And 60
    At Robert Johnson's Grave, Greenwood, MS... 61
    If I ever met Peter Wolf 62
    When I remember That Joni Mitchell Too Has Allodynia 63
    I heard Lead Belly and Blind Lemon on the Street where I was born.. 64
    Quantum Decoherence 65
    Jerry, Underwater... 67
    Van—the Man... 68
    The *Laughremen* 69

Not Quite Stranded 70

Sources 75
Acknowledgments... 85

Liner Notes

Growing up dyslexic and unable to entertain myself with a book, my world could be oppressively quiet. It could also be deafening loud. My natural tendency towards observations resulted in an incessant stream of reflections and analysis I was constantly making in my own head that had nowhere to go. Attempts to express myself were confined to poorly draw hieroglyphics, or dictations to my younger sister as I created elaborate worlds with our Playmobil characters. Sports helped—the frenetic static of my disquieted mind burning off in competition and camaraderie. So did reaching out into the world to find creative people who could give voice to my personal experiences, like so many others have done before me.

The deepest pool of these voices were in my parent's vast music collection. I loved the private ritual of pursuing the neatly organized stack of tinny plastic, selecting a CD, opening the jewel cases with the hollow percussion of a gentle unclicking, sliding out the liner notes from the four semicircles that kept the booklet in place, and trying to read along as the music played. Alone in my bedroom, I remember the gloss of the liner notes under my fingertips as I traced the lyrics in time, the tight weave of the rug, the marks it made on my elbows as I propped myself up on my stomach, the rubbery spring of the buttons of the remote of my boom box. Reading along to the music was like a homemade book-on-tape. And while I don't equate lyrics to poetry in a one-to-one comparison, I wouldn't have known the poetic power of someone else giving voice to my experience without those lyrics: Bonnie Raitt singing John Prine's "If dreams were lightning/ And thunder were desire/ This old house would've burned down." The unfettered energy and stifled potential I felt was Van Morrison singing, "hey, it's me, I'm dynamite and I don't know why."

I.

If I Ventured in the Slipstream

**The First Draft of *Astral Weeks*,
or The Emotional Labor of Janet "Planet" Rigsbee Morrison**

Janet's at the kitchen table
transcribing raw buds
of someone else's childhood—
bending memories into ghosts
canopies casting shadows
from Orangefield to Bay Street
arguments with her husband's
heroes and home décor—
Janet's at the kitchen table
while little Peter naps? plays?
ignores the harsh silence when
the improvisation stops and his mother
pauses, catches up, rewinds,
plays back, and checks her work.
Janet's at the kitchen table
making her own percussion,
pressing buttons on the tape recorder,
her pen like a púa scrapping a guiro
as she scribbles over paper,
over the linoleum surface in the cramped,
upstairs, subdivided apartment
along the street of trees and haphazard parking,
windows opened to a Cambridge spring.
She's reading it back. She's dreaming down
these avenues, back along the lane
saying what doesn't work. She's not
just a ballerina, a little angel child.
Janet's at her kitchen table
editing her own love song.

At the Langhorne Slim Show, East Side Milwaukee
for Erica

We agree:
Sean's like me.

I tell you about New Jersey's waist,
how it's cinched where Philly nips in.
Maybe you remember a little about
the Delaware River from elementary school—
the Hessian Forces at Trenton the day after Christmas?
This isn't about that.

If New Jersey is a peanut,
I'm from the middle of the top bubble.
Horse country, if you believe it—and you should.
We have the very, very best tomatoes, the sweetest corn,
fireflies sparking like the creation of galaxies
played out in the lens of a backwards telescope.

I'm always painting maps,
traveling the distance
like a parallel rule:
gliding stuttered steps,
saying what is, and what is not, New England,
which only matters to those
who spent a childhood on 95 heading North,
who crave small Bay waves and rock beaches.

We haven't lost the instinct
to count down to summer.
We still shelter in Sinatra
when school feels like a leaded x-ray smock.

So, in this close quartered concert,
when he mentions "Ocean City,"
I'm the only one who cheers.

Between the Viaducts of Your Dreams
for Alyssa

It's colder than you
thought it would be, bare-
foot in a cove. Santa Barbara,
finally feeling like home.

The sand on the top of your feet
dry, but sticking like flour.
Your terrier barks at the waves,
running back to rocks,
iridescent green with algae.

Your mother is there
because mothers are in all dreams.
She dances en pointe to *Ballerina*
but now she's 20,
and the rocks framing the beach

form follies, cathedralling the cove to echo
choral music you sang in Europe

and your father is moved
like the first Christmas
he heard you sing and thought
you can do this, you should do this

and he waltzes with your mother
and your dog barks in time

sweeping you further into sleep.

folklore

I say, there would be no *folklore* without *Astral Weeks*
and Louisa says dads everywhere would click on that—
still unwritten—article and send it to their daughters

as proof from another daughter, that Taylor Swift
is the saltwater taffy that strains the jaw as you eat,
as you decide if you even like waxy sugar. But mostly,

"exile" conjures Door County in September
when one sweater isn't comfort enough after dark
and you need a little Mt. Gay in your cider to observe

the blueness of Vega shining at the top of Lyra
in the astral field. And who doesn't need to scream
into waves at Cave Point as lake water touches

bottom, crests, and crashes loudly against the cliffs?
The music plays and even the branches come alive
in their seasonal decay—anthocyanin edging tree leaves

as you sip craft cocktails at Wickman House, floral
notes of Death's Door gin like John Payne on flute
riding on top of the tune, smooth as goat milk soap.

Wasn't the whole city of Milwaukee disappointed
when Bon Iver didn't address the crowd ten years
after *For Emma*? Like Van at the Hollywood Bowl,

seeking protection from the loneliness of the crowd,
walking on as the band's already playing, not speaking
but strumming? Wasn't Orpheus himself pulled apart?

Beside You
> *standing with my sister Brett*

The minister will say, "marriage is like a boat,"
when he means, being married is like being at sea:
sublime between doldrums, between squalls.
In your magic shroud you breathe in
you breathe out you breathe in you breathe out
the bright smell of peonies. My arms will shake
under the weight of your hanging dimpled-rose lilies
as sweat beads under our makeup, in the pointed island breeze,
tears well during the reading from "Genesis—"
> *Wheresoever she was, there was Eden—*

I Shall Watch the Ferryboats and They'll Get High

Jumping hedges is not about
"The Swimmer"

but coming to Greenport
was like sinking,

like lifting a veil
or reverse engineering déjà vu:

the ferries passing each other,
bow thrusters gargling like garbage disposals,

docking with the spongy give of the wooden pilings
the treated wood, wet and greening.

Enter starboard: the love interest,
joint between his lips,

breaking a beer bottle overboard with a winch handle.
And me:

back against the lifelines,
fingers waxy from whipping twine.

For Bob, at Ben's Wedding
with references to Jane Hirschfield's "Tree" and the Grateful Dead

The immensities tapping at our lives
aren't always green—
they are holes:
footprints in the duff
where sorrel doesn't grow.
They ripple through every moment
in involuntary caught breaths:
in the gold of sunshine
of an early June afternoon:
sweat trickling down our backs.

I haven't written enough poems
or sailed across the Atlantic
like we promised we would

but Lisa says,
my painting of *American Beauty*
is close at hand

and when the band strikes up
"Friend of the Devil"
we all get up and dance.

Sam Cooke is on the Radio and the Night is Filled With Space
    for Lenea Claire Grace

On the road to Omaha
I sent you
Rick Danko and
Richard Manuel
singing, "Bring it on Home to Me,"
back when they were still
Levon and The Hawks.

I'm not nostalgic.
I'm falling out of orbit,

meditating badly.

Lenea,
Rick Danko's middle
name was Clare

and for May
this rain is still
too cold.

Fret Noise

Greil Marcus argues that everyone swoons
over *Astral Weeks* but real connoisseurs
cite *Veedon Fleece* as their favorite Van album
when they want to act superior than their friends.

And look, I find myself Googling the word
for the sound fingers make sliding
down the strings of a bowed guitar neck,
like swollen wood expanding in summer humidity
piping backing in a door jam,
or feedback whining through speakers,
or Merry Clayton in "Gimme Shelter."

I fall into the trap, saying something like,
Raymond Carver never cut off a short story
quicker or with less resolution than
"Linden Arden Stolen the Highlights."

I find myself bragging
that *Pottermore* says an Irish
wolfhound is my patronus.

And to my knowledge
no one has ever treated the line,
"cleaved their heads off with a hatchet,"
with tenderness of a lullaby,
the sanctity of a hymn,

with the urgency that is freed
from his belly like a controlled demolition
like he's always just fallen
out of love and is battling gravity

the way satellites use centripetal force
or kestrels hover over air that others can't see
are flowing torrents.

Still, if you want to impress me, show a little courage.
Cite *No Guru, No Method, No Teacher.*
The Healing Game. What's Wrong With this Picture?

Between the Viaducts of Your Dreams
for Dad

You don't dream.
You walk,

collecting lampshades,
stacking them in corners.

You scare your wife
lifting paintings off

the wall above the bed,
rocky on the mattress.

You walk to check
the anchor line

of the apartment
to see if it's dragging.

You walk, except
for that one time

you were climbing sequoias
with Jack Nicklaus

and I wanted to say to you,
was it really your father

with you in the
Redwood Tree?

It smells like rain,
maybe even thunder.

And It Stoned Me, Prelude

Once in the Reina Sofia
        alone, in the white light
                (*white heat*)
I suddenly saw *Guernica*
and I inhaled like a stone
skipping through my rib cage
        thinking, *if I knew Picasso*—
and while it was not my place
to cry, it meant something new
after months of living in Spain
I knew why the upside-down
faces were painted all in gray

It Stoned Me Just Like Going Home

Still,
my hands tremor
too much to be trusted
with the vinyl.

That first summer,
we wore down the diamond,
WASPs at top volume
off key and insistent.

This was once a ballroom,
all thirty by thirty feet resonating

the noise
of not just my childhood:
ice against glass
a sharp edge
a southerly wind
building in the afternoon,
scents of potting soil,
Murphy's Soap and grass,
the cool air of a just-vacuumed room,
open-windowed and doily-covered.

And the warm sugar
of dark liquor
while outside,
the leaves of the cooper beech
block the reflections off the black-night water.
I argue with my dad
about the lights on the tugs,
how long the tow.
And you know my mother—
hardy crackers and a full bar.

Look,
I'm not saying we drink a lot.
I'm saying we're good at it.

I picked *Moondance*
the circumference of the album
traced white into the cardboard sleeve,
liner notes of wood,
hidden butter spirits and far darrigs.

I laid down on the high-pile rug
past tipsy and tired
to a song I've heard hundreds of times
made new

and wept.

How precious and pretentious:
rich, white drunks
with their Van Morrison vinyl.
But it happened
and it was beautiful.

Caught One More Time Up on Cyprus Avenue

If there are versions of ourselves
treading like brushes on cymbals
baring our first names in disguise
walking the slim slow incline of the streets
of our childhood, I'd be in a bucket seat
on 287 staring out of a tinted window,
FM stations preset, L.L. Bean backpack at my feet
bare legs, goose bumping under my uniform kilt.
I'd be in love at eleven with the boy who biked
from River Road to write his name
in hearts in the gravel of my driveway.
That's why I believe, this a grown man is singing
about ghosts, the echoes of rhymes through the years.
How with each step from Hyndford Street
the houses still stretch, gain backyards,
and detach. How it's the roots under
the sidewalks that force the concrete to crack.

Dweller on the Threshold
for Alyssa

I feel guilty I still can't surf

you and your Bloodlife poems
know a dweller on the threshold

is a ghost. A real ghost
to those believers in ghosts.

To me, it seemed as
real as god.

Knowing what's needed
then delivering

is like Shooting the Sun.
My mother taught me

I could always procrastinate
as long as I was writing a poem.

You know that fear
that bubbles up

like foam in the bottle neck
of a tapped beer

when someone asks you
about your "creative process?"

No.
I bet you don't.

The Last Time I was Drunk
      for Tory

I told the wedding band
that they should *not* play
"Shakedown Street."

"But no," they told me,
"everyone loves the Dead."

And I said,
      with the self-assured smugness
      of a drunk person,
"That later disco crap
is not the Dead
at their best.

You should
cover 'Franklin's Tower'
Oooh! Or 'The Mighty Quinn.'

And I know what you're thinking:
it's a Dylan song.
But you know,
the Dead covered it.
They did a great job.
You could too."

It was not
what they were thinking.

**The Sweet Inspirations,
or In Defense of "Brown Eyed Girl"**

How many listening know that it's
Cissy Houston singing? *Sha la la la la*
just like that?

Or that Russ Savakus used a pick
to pluck his bass for added
punctuation during the bridge

like the pointed discs of river rock
on the footbridge over the Beechie
that runs the whole length of The Hollow
behind the row houses of Abetta Parade?
How there are the holes where the stones
have been kicked loose from the mortar,
how like childhood, something is gone
but a depression remains?

While Walking Routinely to and From Work

> I have wasted my life.
> —James Wright, "Lying in a Hammock at William Duffy's Farm in Pine Island, Minnesota"

There is always the possibility that it ⇧ is a triumphant statement. That a life wasted in a field (*the fields the fields are always wet with rain after a summer shower*) of sunlight between two pines, with nothing to show for it but poems, is an accomplishment.

More likely, it's a self-defeating, horrifying realization that unravels and undermines the stacked up, idyllic images before it. We readers relate to feeling that way. And of course, we don't believe him. Not after reading the visuals he conjured and experiencing the artistry of his emotional manipulation—to bring us so high, so comforted, in an actual hammock, only to have us crash, winded, into self-pity, completely beat. He's like a seagull flying straight up to drop crabs over rocks to spilt them open. He's Justin Vernon "in Milwaukee, off his feet" insisting, in the middle of all his well-crafted genius, that, "at once I knew I was not magnificent," and us readers thinking:

No. I'm not magnificent.

No. I have wasted my life.

Adam Duritz gets it. He reminds listeners, and by listeners, I mean, me—insistently:

> You don't want to waste your life, now darlin'
> Oh, you don't want to waste your life.

And as if anticipating my question—how? how do I avoid ending up like James Wright—but my god, wouldn't it be great to be as magnificent [a writer] as James Wright—Duritz advise the following, with similar resolve:

> Change.
> Change.
> Change.
> Change.
> Change.

Change.
Change.
Change.
Change.

And I should.
I wake up in these heavy mornings,
buckling under the volume of too much
caught water, too many held breaths.
Like the tide's predictable and incremental
movements, I'm never at home and
everywhere there are people
making things harder for themselves,
brought to a boil and whistling
back to themselves, steam settling on
the sides of sticky cupboards. To John,
I admit I drive 80 in a 65, but how is it
I'm still not there yet, while all around
me I get passed by people going 50?
Change. Change. Change. *Chain of fool[s]*.
John asks, "have you ever in your life
just quit something?" And while the answer
is "yes," his point is, "don't waste your life."

Dwelling

> Let me go down to the water
> Watch the great illusion drown
> —Van Morrison, "Dweller on the Threshold"

I'm sorry. Once
on the east side of the Mystic River
I was kissed carefully
and painted a dining set
and everyone should feel that way forever.

Now, we watch this weak water.
I get too distracted
by the crashes
up against the rocks.

I apologize
for talking too much
in this story,
in the text messages to Lenea afterwards,
for spelling this out through shadow puppets,
for not lying sooner or better.
I've said I'm sorry
by now at least once
to just about everyone.

There's more.
Isn't there always?
I'm trying to say:

This isn't it. This isn't it.
Lenea knows,
I'm a diagnostician.
not a poet.
You tell me to listen to
Live at the Grand Opera House Belfast
in the too closeness of the car,
but I talk to my dog
in high pitches.

It's time to say goodbye
to Lake Michigan,
to let these delusions drown.

Warren Zevon Poems
for Dan Stein

Alyssa called it the Treehouse:
the studio on East 13th
with the stove-sink-fridge
that had to be defrosted weekly,
where we had adult bunk beds
and the yorkie killed the mouse

and there was duct tape residue
on the window from the reinforced X
put in place ahead of Hurricane Sandy

and my cut crystal wine glasses
I inherited from my sister
that I didn't forget, but never retrieved,
when I moved out on Halloween.

All of that happened between A and B, Dan.
On East 13th, I played Alyssa the first
of hundreds of classic rock songs, thanks to you
and your Warren Zevon poems. Who knew
I had a friend who had never heard
"Werewolves of London"?

"Accidentally Like a Martyr" sits
alphabetically at the top
of my music library, plays
automatically in my car—
after such a long, long time,
I now think of salons in the Treehouse,
the escargot I never ate at Loup.

Meditating to Madame George
for Kelsey

Our legs swelled,
our heads, full of pressure

from moderate aging
or a barometric depression

stewing offshore. I gave
her a pattern to breath in.

Our backs, on the teak of the porch,
legs on the railing, L-shaped

to drain the blood and—after
awhile—I pressed play. Then

we breathed how we wanted
only now, it was slower.

On Being Pharrell but Probably Not Being Pharrell
for Su and for Karisa

At the end of the year
there'll be a quiz

on all the members of the Band,
we joke.

Those late-night texts:
saying—not asking—
am I a good poet.
am I good.

At dinner I explain
who George Martin was.
I have another Dewar's
and talk about close micing
drums on *Sgt. Pepper's,*
which is not a new observation.

It's not my observation.

You ask about Ringo
and instead of answering,
I talk about Pete Best.
Am I good?
I sound obnoxious.

Those late night texts:
Here:
Look what Levon's old girlfriend said,
     look what Libby said,
"they were all busy
living up to the story of the Band
and the whole Dylan myth."

I don't wannabe Bob Dylan.
I want to be someone
just a little more happy.

II.

Turn Up Your Radio

Greenwich Mean Time

> My little girl I can't find
> She's five hours behind
> —Bell and Sebastian, "Chickfactor"

Because you're still trying
to impress me, you order a Dalwhinnie,
show me Stuart Murdoch on the mural.

Meantime, there's another Nor'easter
battering through the summer screens.
More spray-stained Pollocks
on the double paned windows.

Five hours from now, I advise:
fold yourself into that feeling:
sink down easily into it like a flat stone
falling through water, the slight friction
of sobriety slowing you down.
The amber liquor like little embers
flaring inside.

You tell me the sunset's glowing orange in Glasgow
but in the photos, it just looks blue.

Bill Remembers Watkins Glen

The summer I built the covered wagon,
I went to Watkins Glen in Stuart Barringer's convertible,
ran into Wendy in the traffic of seventeen-year-olds
migrating towards an experience
we were all too young for at Woodstock.

At the show, I stood in the 600,000
under clouds raining color and smoke and men:
floating circus tents, feathers against the wind.
The sound from the delay towers like the energy
of Cavern Cascade spitting vapor into the atmosphere.
Music, just the landscape: a fairytale vehicle for mescaline.

Heading home, we stopped at the state park,
skinny dipped in clear cool crystal waterfalls
and learned later, a skydiver caught fire
on the way down to the ground.

Wendy Remembers Watkins Glen

It was a miracle I found Bill
at the base of the Finger Lakes
—those stretchmarks on the map.
I had driven to Summer Jam
with my boyfriend Tommy in his white Toyota,
but with this tent made out of garbage bags and duct tape,
I had to literally decamped to Bill's proper tent.

No. I don't remember the impromptu
sound checks, two hours of "Sugaree."
I remember my crush on Gregg Allman,
waiting in line at the porta potties,
the choruses of "mescaline, mescaline"
sung to a tune of a hammock swaying,
the pendulum chirp of black-capped chickadees.

Stuart Remembers Van Morrison and Janis Joplin at the Cole Auditorium, University of Maryland, Friday, June 19, 1970

Maybe it was Bang Records?
Some Bert Berns affiliation
that booked the two acts together.
We were there for Janis.

Van looked past the audience in a dispassionate stance,
his voice spilling from his mouth like the bell of a sax
internal, divine bellows giving him air, growl, grit.
Three or four songs into his set, his tongue got tied.
He started on a loop, something from *Moondance*.
"It's too late to stop now?" His wounds as wide
as an open door. And rather than following
        all his mystic revelations like water trapped
           in a bucket spinning and spinning and spinning
           and spinning,
the crowd started booing—
not savvy or Irish enough to throw pennies.
It's too late to stop now? He exited stage left.

Janis, just days before heading to the Festival Express,
was a relief, her voice, an aura, doubling her being.

Annotated Listening: "Live at the Grand Opera House Belfast"

On the cover, the Grand Opera House Belfast, lit at dusk—but with midday clouds above—is framed so lonely it seems like the only thing there. No people, no cars, which in 1983, I don't know, there might not have been, with all the parking bans inside the city limits. It's as if someone shouted, "mystical rapture!" and with life sucked away, the theatre was left with the lights on, abandoned to house human memories.

Outside of photographs, both then and now, the Opera House stands on Great Victoria Street, smaller than the cosmopolitan buildings that have grown up like steel weeds around it, ambitious to cast shadows over the A1. There are so many cars and buses and people, so many people that they ignore the red brick, the three white circular eyes on its face, that it may well be as lonely as the album cover suggests.

And it's enclosed in a green marble border, like it's standing up at the U.N. general assembly, making a case for peace.

*

"She Gives Me Religion," a prodigious, if not explicit, metaphor. She gives me…"religion." Understood. And in case you missed it, Mark Isham's trumpet solo at 2:45 really…drives it home.

Any crudeness is tempered with church bells and praise, set in a familiar scene: a mystic avenue on a summer Sunday, an organ humming like breath over a coke bottle. It's a walking tune that swaggers, hips on bungee cords. All this pales to his voice as he growls the opening line, allowing his own heart to break in awe so no listeners' has to. After just one line the crowd screams with applause. He mumbles a seamless, "thank you." But what he means is: "you're welcome."

*

Speaking of religion, "Full Force Gale" is a notoriously religious track from this whole Holy Roller phase—but don't count it out as Christian rock. Especially in this recording, even though the audience claps along with energy that could rival any revival meeting.

The song is about being saved from your own dark place, getting out of your cranky sullenness, your most desperate moments, much to your own surprise. He does that with the tender imagery of "whispering shade of trees," against the juxtaposition of vitality, and dare I say, the fun of the tune. It's unexpected, which adds to the pay off. And again, speaking of juxtapositions, the central, startling metaphor, takes the danger of a gale and transforms it into an act of mercy, into a parachute. Also, that horn section! It demands exclamation marks! It's like speeding backwards into a double salchow.

*

"Rave on, John Donne," heavily packed with poetic allusions from Mr. Yeats to Omar Khayyam, may be better read on the printed page than "sung" over anemic woodwinds. Perhaps, that's why Van opts to talk through the first half of the song. He strives not to beat these poets at their own game, but meet them at it:

> *In the moss borne dark dank pools*
> *Rave on, down through the industrial revolution*
> *Empiricism, atomic and nuclear age*

This is certainly true until 4:20 into this 9-minute song. You would be forgiven for slipping ahead. Though if you stick it out, you'd get to hear about Walt Whitman until the speed picks up to a fist-pumping Springsteen pace. New Jersey is full of heroes. Don't skip that. This sequel to "Summertime in England," his acknowledgment of the voices in his head, the salute to his band.

*

"Cleaning Windows" is another sparkling, allusion-filled staple off of his second most recent studio album, *Beautiful Vision*. It goes down much easier than "Rave on, John Dunne," but this live version isn't particularly blowin' your mind! It's trying to decide if it wants to be jazz, or do an American country twangy thing in the beginning, ironically staying far away from the stripped down Delta Blues he's referencing. Further confusing the presentation, he plays tug-o-war with the accompanying vocalists and the game ends in a draw. But it's fine. It's fun. Some songs can bare the weight of a lack of restraint.

*

The local audience never doesn't cheer when he sings, "in the County Down" during "Northern Musie."

*

Honorable mention goes to "Beautiful Vision," which grows on me. I never use to think of it as spectacular. Its easy blues too predictable and uncomplicated, its lyrics too sentimental, but then I end up listening to it all the way through anyway. It's not just that I don't skip the track. It's that I go to skip it, then stop.

The same can be said for "Vanlose Stairway."

*

Lastly, the most triumphant track is, "Dweller on the Threshold." This is why music is preformed live. At first listen, you might not think the studio recoding could be improved upon: the deep throated sax ghostly shadowing the lyrics, the persistent play on the hi-hat propelling the song like a train on tracks. But live, at the Grand Opera House, Van stokes that fire, speeds up that train. He leads the charge and as the band blends together with the zeal of the crowd. They match his intensity while he retains his solitude, issuing this imperative: "Lift me up, consume my darkness." His plea is met only with the gentle cooing of his backing vocalists.

Katie Kissoon, Lady Bianca, and Carol Kenyon echo, spot, anticipate, support, which isn't always the case in some of his overly-produced albums that follow this period, where the women's voices are afterthought ornaments, imposed on top of a final take, rather than true partners. Here, they are like the horns, in conversation with our front man, highlighting, answering, voicing the inarticulate speech of the heart.

Van's is a subtle vocal performance—not performance—emotional experience. In one song he goes through stages of pure confidence, resigns himself to defeat, anguish, resilience. He draws out syllables like he's tearing the fabric of his soul. He's the embodiment of a spirit occupying two spaces, stuck, despite his immense power. He's Janus, facing both directions at once. He's a Northern Irishman. living in America. playing in Belfast.

From Forest Hills Stadium, September 12, 2018

Jessica Hopper suggests we put "Sweet Thing" on repeat
and see who cries first. This, and other *Astral Weeks* alchemy,
screams from the screaming cover of

THE FIRST COLLECTION OF CRITICISM BY A LIVING
   FEMALE ROCK CRITIC

But if I was playing Sweet-Thing-Chicken,
I'd be bowled over from the first stretched-out *I*:
a vow that lengthens the listener's shadow:
pulls and releases with the grace of an unsnapped elastic,
accommodating our cosmic duality

**What *Pet Sounds* Means to Me,
or Franklin and I Go See Brian Wilson**
        for Franklin

Franklin's always up here.
Like, way, way up here
vibrating with

frenetic joy

and neither one of us finishes a story

before the next thought,
next song.

We both know
an above average amount
about Blondie Chaplin.

Franklin says the way I love my dog
says a lot about me.
I say, "East coast girls are hip."

I want to teach Franklin to swim
so when I say
how things sound
underwater—dreamvoices reverberating—

how everything's stained glass,
light playing in constant motion,

how on my back,
with water in my ears,
the sun, watchful and guiding,
I feel the most full—
the negative fluid pressure off of my lungs,
weightless in the salt,

how shallow water blackouts
are scarier than sharks,

he'd get me.

III.

Old Old Woodstock

Dominique in Woodstock, NY, 1967

I want to shout,
je m'ennuie but
my lashes are long enough
that I never make eye contact
and the trees are tall enough,
there's no horizon.
Sometimes I still
wear ribbons in my hair
or the white t-strap mary janes
I was married in. I don't

say, *je suis agité. Je me sens pris au piège*—
the birches branching like picket fences—
that overlooking the Ashokan Reservoir—
I just see more trees. Janet sits

on the forest floor reading palms,
but my company are cats,
cocktails, sometimes Sara.
The days are mostly nights
which are mostly noise,

the sunlight has so far to go
to come down
through the leaves. But
to *Rolling Stone*,
here to talk to the boys,
I say, "There's nothing here

but dope,
music,
and beauty. If
you're a woman,
and you don't make music
and you don't use dope,

there's nothing here at all."

Imagining West Saugerties

It started with *Jericho,*
"Max" painted into the clouds,
touchable edges from the brush
cresting in traceable tracks.

I realize:
the house isn't as pink
as Peter painted it.
It's not as big as they claimed.

The basement
should smell like weed
but instead, smells like a basement:
air cool, dusty,
a slight dampness living in carpets
laid down for the acoustics.

Not stagnant
but suspended
not as if in amber,
but like photographs in liner notes,

as if Richard Manuel,
never having died,
could make me laugh
with awkward, gentle sweetness

and I could step outside
away from the rockabilly warm up
into the light and chlorophyll woods
chiming with daytime cricket static.

4% Pantomime

The difference between Johnnie Walker Red
and Johnnie Walker Black
is the register of two baritones
in compliment, not competition,
because, after all Richard—
        oh, Richard—
said Van was his responsibility
to drive home through old, old Woodstock
back to the place where he himself use to live.
Richard said he could drive with his eyes closed
he said, in a psychic rebuttal to Blind Faith—
        well, I'm wasted and I can't find my way home—

Here's what we know:
it was winter in Ulster County, NY
Van slipped on the ice behind the car,
Beak behind the wheel, mercifully in park.
We also know:
Van improvised the lyrics
        a tongue-and-cheek-melodrama,
           his first lyrical complaint about the biz.

We don't know what they talked about
or even if they sang in the car,
headlights bouncing off the snow,
if Richard played the wheel like keys
wrists pulsing like kneading dough
if Belfast Cowboy could hear phantom
hammers falling on strings.
It was a gas, it was a smash.
Oh, Richard.
Oh, Richard—

Van at *The Last Waltz*

Enough has been said of the high kicks,
the bedazzled maroon leisure suit,
Allen Toussaint's horn arrangement
        turning up and up
turning around a tryptophan crowd,
heavy with frost and fairwells—

Preserved in black and white,
        not the Scorsese special 35mm,
is Van ambling on mid "Tura Lura Lural"
the way a feather floats in an updraft
before he opens his mouth
and kindling sparks the fuelwood
in the ether for a crackling warmth.
Where was this lullaby in the final cut?
Or Diane DiPrima or Robert Duncan
and the other poetry performances?

In the final number it is Rick who whispers
repeatedly to Van in his stage fright,
who points him under the middle chandelier
to the central mic.

Morrison and Dylan Perform "Foreign Window"

They both were singing about Rimbaud
which is just a placeholder for *poetry*,
for *deeper than pop* and *radio play,*
for not making enough eye contact

but like the phases of the moon,
each exists in a stage of becoming,
pulling tides and growing more
and more into their icon shapes.

Yet here, everyone can see
what I have been saying:
this holy well inside him
this geyser at the surface:

Van Morrison is a lunar halo

whose full voice casts light,
not Alice Bailey nonsense.
He is a round moonbow
to Dylan's sharp crescent.

He is steel coiled on a tuning key
in the injured atmosphere,
in the shadow of the Acropolis,
under the weight of myth

and his own expectations.
He is getting close and never
arriving. He is at the edge
of space, filling every corner.

IV.

Looking for the Veedon Fleece

A Mischief of Two
for Matty

Dublin smells like evaporations,
roasted barely, and Butler's Chocolates.
As we round Merrion Park and the statue
of heavyweight champ Oscar Wilde,
the bouquet of pine and white mulberry
overcomes the tar of cigarettes.
You salute the magpies and don't
recall the rhyme. We're sharing
an umbrella, and I remember
where I learned to count crows:
"One for sorrow. Two for joy."

Looking for the Veedon Fleece

From Limerick I went on to Spanish Point.
The dunes rolled down between the headlands
into surf breaks and curved pockets of coast
where stones bit through the sand like dorsal fins,
the parallel lines of incoming waves forming
their own geometry against ancient sediment.

At cocktail hour, there were hardly colors,
the lingering sunlight put a veil over the banks.
Maybe it was sea spray or the wind
kicking up silt in the links, the air full
of particle reflections, turning everything
a glow, without definition, casting
Country Clare in gold and gray.

But by the time I got to Bellaghy
and was confronted with "Postscript:"

> *along the Flaggy Shore…when the wind*
> *And the light are working off each other*
> *So that the ocean on one side is wild*

I wanted to sink into the Atlantic.
You don't push the river.

William Blake and the Eternals?
Seamus Heaney?
You don't push the river!

But you don't pull no punches.
I was there: the air smelled of sheep
and alfalfa, instead kelp, it was alive
with apparitions of wrecked Armada sailors.
I was watching surfers at sunset,
feeding myself on soup and brown bread.

And when I had turned the corner
and saw eleven swans improbably flying,
like a broken Christmas song,
in the lee of the Mourne Mountains
wings as white as canvas sails,
necks like reaching struts,

I ran flatfooted, heels slamming
the whole width of Tyrella Beach
packed hard as cement,
pitted from razor clams
until I was deep enough in the Irish Sea
to sting my skin purple.

The Streets of Arklow

smelled of burnt rubber
when I tried to back up
with the parking brake on,

uphill and backwards into
left-hand traffic across from
Taurus's Chinese Take Away.

Other than that, the streets of Arklow
were pleasantly underwhelming:
Paddy Power, P. Power's Souvenir Shop,

a library, the need for new paint,
contributing to the feeling that actual people
live along the banks of the Avoca River.

Arklow wasn't Dalkey—
gated and ccTVed
to protect the mansions.

Or Killarney, playing dress up
with itself for the benefit
of retirees in coaches

—for my benefit.

Blue on blue and green on gold
bunting remained strung up outside pubs,
alternatively bleached out in the sun

then wet with rain,
the Kerry-Dublin match
having just ended in a draw

reminding me to look up
the rules to Gaelic football
or Google Stephen Cluxton.

As I walked the streets
of Arklow to the dark teal
of The Brook House for Guinness,

to the bridge for a view of the masts
in the harbor I never made it to
and back along the Riverwalk trail

before I sat in St. Mary's park to write,
I thought, how could one's head be *full
of poetry* here? In this ordinary life?

Unless poetry is always in your head:
lines that bubble up like oxygen
escaping mud at the bottom of a lake.

Box of Rain
for my Dad, on the death of Robert Hunter

Rain coming sounds like tires on gravel, the starting
up of a band saw. It brings out the smell of dressed
salad without ripping into leaves: no green leaf
volatiles scattered into the air. On Ballycander
Road where everyone has a story of Van in Holywood,
the rain smells the same, sounds the same,
as it does on Joliet Street where my father
lows like thunder only dogs can hear.

Purple Heather

In the hefty knit of my sweater,
I can still smell the lanolin in the fibers,
the clinging Clifden rain—

memories stick like rust
color stains on white porcelain
from the peaty water,

hazy as the Connor Pass
completely fogged in
in the wind and the rain.

When the leaves come falling down.
Thoor Ballylee looms,
not in height but in the mind,

through every gorse-covered
mountain road: the tower
we are all toiling under

a cold shadow on a golden
autumn day: the aster weeks,
late season blooms.

Northern Ireland Poetry

> I've been living in another country
> That operates along entirely different lines
> —Van Morrison, "Got to Go Back"

In the title page of *The Last Peacock*
Gerald Dawe, signed "Jerry"

like I had been initiated
by the dozen or so traffic circles

coming down from Downpatrick
on the way to Bangor,

or my proper pronunciation
of "Newtownards,"

and he wrote,
"RAVE ON!"

smiled at me and said,
"You'll know what it means."

Rave on in a voice,
in a shapeless flame.

Rave on through time and space
forming memories like decaying

sphagnum in a blanket bog,
like stones stacked in a passage tomb.

So I drank wine with Leslie
back home at the River Mill,

read our own work aloud.
Paul drove me through Ardglass

I confronted the sameness—the oneness—
of fishing boats docked there and in Newport.

Facing Coney Island (baby) I thought about,
when he was a young boy back in Orangefield—

and hated everything that wasn't weeds
growing in the garden of his wild mind,

like me at Peck under the glass of imagined
greenhouses, waiting out the winter.

Queens of the Slipstream
for Tenley at Greens

In Sligo, far across the sea,
I changed awkwardly in a rental car
tiptoed over the ostrich egg rocks
that rubbed together like grinding teeth
as they rolled before they wore down
into sand at Rosses Point Beach.
There were two other women swimming
in the stinging September water.
While in Jamestown I knew,
there are women posed
on diving boards springing
first to fall further.

Ways of Looking at "Foreign Window"

The spines of my books
look like crow's feet:
lines of wisdom crushed
into the paper housing
my collected consciousness.
Across continental divides,
I carry these books
stuffed into suitcases,
slouched, water damaged.
We all have reasons for moving.
Now I'm free to roam, everywhere I go
I feel like I'm home.

*

I no longer know how to pray
but I was reading on the sofa,
I was singing every prayer.
I was singing, choking,
face turning hot, wet cheeks,
talking back in the margins,
yawing muscles in blue ink.

*

I spied her from the foreign window
walking her dog, such a pedestrian act
for the herbalist next door who dances naked
at the Ballynoe Stone Circle on the solstice.

*

Running down the autumn road,
the blackface sheep skitter
like a murmuration of blackbirds.

*

I slept through the dawn chorus.

*

I made friends with the Kerry cattle
I could not see from out of my window
but drank from the stream that ran through the garden
where, if I couldn't write, I could read.

*

I had gone down to Lake Geneva
cradling ideas of *This Side of Paradise,*
which only made me feel pride in the Cliff Walk.
Maybe I missed the salt water and sailboats?

O, says Rimbaud, let me go into the sea!

*

Oh man! says Byron, thou feeble tenant of an hour!

*

If you get it right this time,
there's no need to revise.
Driving all night chasing some mirage,
tell the folks back home:
this is the promised land calling
and I'm not looking for Tír na nÓg.

*

The hills aren't green but a patchwork
of purple and yellow heather past its bloom,
where the wind comes up and scatters
powdery white buds like moths over the road way,
where the doors to the monastic city are twelve feet up
but we are all forgiven because we ask to be.

*

"Homesick" means the opposite
of what it should.

*

This window is a mirror.
Make me down a pallet on the floor
where my thought's escaping,
where my music's playing,
where I can bed down on my own,
vertiginous and hypotensive.
Make me a horizon so I never need another.

V.

Still for Searching for the Philosopher's Stone

And

by beginning a song
with a conjunction
everyone, everyone
can tell a thought
began long before
music started:
a glad tiding
that connects
like a strand
of polymers across
his catalog. And
with this device
he isn't just borrowing
from the Bible:
he is writing his own.

At Robert Johnson's Grave, Greenwood, MS
for Lenea

Water seeped up from the earth

      bleeding the Little Tallahatchie River,

tipping over tombstones,
splitting them in two.

The sunset paused,
      the still air, orange
or in shadow stretching

over an April green.
As we picked our way through puddles

there was no breeze,
no mosquitoes,

just an immobile irrigation rig
spanning the soy field
on the other side of Money Road

      hypnotic rows of seedlings,
      lines of forced perspective

      heading towards unincorporated towns.
Against the paling sky,

tree limbs looked like spider webs
      or fingertips,

giants casting shade
over the graveyard.

And when we turned to leave,
      stepping gingerly on the soggy grass,
mud splattered across my back

either telling me to stay,
or hurrying me away.

If I ever met Peter Wolf

my opening line would be something like,
>*My dad went to the same high school as J. Geils,*

something to prove I'm relevant,
that our lives are connected by a web of the universe:
spider silk that's only visible when sunlight hits it at the right time of day,
strong on a microscopic level, if easily brushed away.

It would feel like trespassing to tell him the deeper truth:
> that his friendship with Van is a redemptive breeze off the Charles River
>> on a mild spring afternoon,
>
> that I imagine him in '68 with his recording equipment,
> that I have heard the bootleg of The Van Morrison Controversy at The
>> Catacombs,
>
> that the mundane birth of *Astral Weeks* just makes it less mythical,
>> not less magical,
>
> that we should all be shouting at wild crowds,

This is the man who wrote "Gloria!"

When I Remember That Joni Mitchell Too Has Allodynia

I part my hair down the middle,
make blonde curtains, wings folding over my cheekbones
in solidarity and as a small reminder,
> that there is part of my body that doesn't feel,
> that I too, am more than this body,
> that if I felt less, I'd be a better person,
> that Joni is naked somewhere in British Columbia,
> paying too much for heat,
> trying to stay warm and not let anything touch her.

I heard Lead Belly and Blind Lemon on the Street where I was born
for Tyehimba Jess

Whenever I see white surfaces—
boat hulls and buildings—
glowing orange,
the sinking sun somewhere behind me,
I think of the Delta in April
just before, I imagine, it becomes
a sweating mosquito swamp den.

I allowed myself to be distracted
by the misspelling of Lead Belly.
but certain sunsets remind me of Greenwood,
the ones that last a beat too long—
the air, on fire, resisting night.

Quantum Decoherence

Tom Petty is unreliable
as a narrator. Do we really
believe he doesn't miss her?

Through the butterscotch
scented Jeffrey Pines,
I glide up Coldwater Canyon
to Mulholland thanks
to the uninterrupted ease

of my continuously variable transmission,
its conical ingenuity—a wonder,
second only to the Bluetooth
conducting quanta in airwaves
or ether—mechanized
music of the spheres.

A physicist will tell you
the moon itself is in free fall:
a predictable trajectory
that reads like a mixed metaphor.

I thought the Valley was a thirsty place,
burnt from a lack of ozone and condescension
from shadier zip codes with bay figs and kumquats,

but here I really drive west down Ventura Boulevard,
the trumpet trees in their Barbie pink
reminding me of cherry blossoms, of northeast springs,
that the address on my licenses has never matched

the address on my lease, that quantum mechanics
can unambiguously tell you where a body will be—
or at least the probability where it will be
and maybe even then, a little off to the side.

Heisenberg thought nothing exists in space
until you look at it. Was I only visiting
this mythology until I rode my brake down

the backside of the Canyon, seeing the vapor
that had risen off the Pacific and got trapped
in the puckered folds of the mountains?
What a pity they call this smog.

Further south, bells are ringing
for the return of the swallows.
It's a reminder that migration
also means to come back home.

Jerry, Underwater
for me

The heat inside
isn't from a furnace,
fueling chronic aches.

It's the work of cells,
somehow still doing
the mindless labor of living,

warming the thin layer
of water around your skin,
trapped like an aura,

in the snug compression
of neoprene, in turn,
warming you, in the cradle

of neutral buoyancy.
Here, sound moves faster.
Exhaling is a valve release

a friendly tumbling of bubbles
that tickle your cheeks, not
a series of metronomic moans.

Here, it all doesn't hurt so bad.

Van—the Man

The musician
builds brick
and concrete
soundscapes
under shaded wood,
along craggy shores,
seen through
the curtain
of a mystic fog
and shattered light.

The man circles
his own beautiful
vison: pulled in
then slingshot back
out into deep space
in magnetic conjunction
with his warbled reflection,
tapping at the glass,
leaving spider cracks
on the now cut veneer.

The *Laughremen*

> Most notable of these are the *laughremen*, fairies found only in south Armagh [in Northern Ireland], who are surly and have an unsociable disposition. The laughre men guard hoards of hidden gold and their sole purpose is to drive away inquisitive strangers.
> —Bob Curran, *A Field Guide to Irish Fairies*

I've been living with a *laughremen*
and the nasty things spat from his lips
in fits of contempt,

swallowing shards of broken
daydreams splintering inside me
as I digest doubt for days.

I can feel his cheeks burning
red with each inquiry: "Why?
Why, must I always explain?"

I have been living with this fairy
engulfed under his king tides
breathing through my gills,

leeching off his magic, drinking
the iron in his blood, bitter
as cruciferous vegetables,

sharp and bright as tinsel.
I've been living with a fairy.
I've been dancing in his shadow.

Not Quite Stranded

While I might not have been in the exact emotional state of Lester Bangs, "nerves shredded and ghosts and spiders looming and squatting across the mind," there was a time I too compulsively hunkered down under the ephemeral comfort of Van Morrison's *Astral Weeks*.

In 2015, I was working in marketing and content development for a high-end yacht builder. The work environment was toxic. I was over-worked yet under-utilized, then I'd limp home for a few more hours of writing and editing poetry, hoping to at least find some sense of accomplishment or relief in a creative outlet. This, as my entire nervous system rebelled against me in all manner of indignations, courtesy of a chronic illness.

Unlike Bangs, I was doing everything I could think of to improve my situation, but no amount of doctors' appointments, or submitting to journals, or job applications, or dates, seemed to change anything. I felt like a gnat, dying of thirst on flypaper, trapped and forgettable.

When the sense of doom boiled over, I'd get up from my desk at the Melville Marina District in Portsmouth, Rhode Island to get content for a social media post. I'd walk out among the boats, trying to lose myself in the forest of masts. I would press up against the railing there like the crowds at the Battery in Herman Melville's "Loomings" peering waterwards, only unlike Ishmael in *Moby Dick*, and unlike an early version of myself, I would not be going to sea, despite the "damp, drizzly November in my soul." I had no choice but to find another escape so I turned to *Astral Weeks*. If I had to cut a video for YouTube, I'd plug in my headphones to handle the audio, when the truth was, the audio was on mute and I was venturing into the slipstream. More and more, those eight tracks of *Astral Weeks* became my security blanket, my companion as I composed a blog post or prepared for a boat show.

This type of relationship with the album seems common among Van fans. In 1978, a decade after *Astral Weeks* was released, Bangs wrote his iconic review of the album for the Greil Marcus-edited anthology *Stranded: Rock and Roll for a Desert Island*. In it, Bangs declared *Astral Weeks* was "the rock record with the most significance in my life so far." Marcus himself claims, "I've played *Astral Weeks* more than I've played any other record I own." Similarly, musician and author Ryan H. Walsh claims *Astral Weeks* is his "favorite record of all time." Walsh writes when he first encountered the record, "I was experiencing my first true heartbreak—I felt like a shell of myself, carved out by loneliness." Rock journalist Jessica Hopper recommends "Astral Weeks," the album's title track for "when the chasm of human experience feels unbridgeable… and there is no absolution to be had, no forgiveness to salve you, and the world feels too much in its infinite newness and it's midnight and people are screaming and feeding babies ranch-flavor chicken fingers from a bucket." Stifled, sad people seem to gravitate towards *Astral Weeks*.

Bangs writes that, "It sounded like the man who made *Astral Weeks* was in terrible pain," which is why he, Bangs, connected with the album so intensely during his own time of turmoil. And yes, Van Morrison, both the man and his public persona—if there even is one—is, to use his own words, "a gaping wound that will never heal." Morrison is wounded from being an only child, from being deeper than everyone else around him, from being a loner, from watching loved ones die in his youth, from prejudice, from being screwed over in the music industry, from an overdeveloped sense of injustice, from it-doesn't-matter-quite-frankly-and-it's-none-of-our-business-anyway, as he keeps telling us.

The appeal of *Astral Weeks* isn't just that misery loves company; it's that the work legitimizes the listeners' feelings and carves out a respite. There are more heartbreaking records to listen to, but *Astral Weeks* effectively repairs pain and knits back together what was broken. Are you lonely? "I'll stand beside you." Because I'm worried about the same thing, "If I ventured…Could you find me?" We're listening, so the implied answer is, "yes." Yes, take us "strongly in your [song] again and we will not remember that we ever felt the pain." The passion in Morrison's voice, the desperation he conveys, the depth of his conviction and anguish and love, validates our feelings of despair—just as it is validating to read that Ishmael involuntarily pauses before coffin warehouses. It made my frustration towards mergers and cubicles and overly stuffed, communal office refrigerators feel justified. The music connected me to a greater sense of creativity and purpose that was slipping away from me in my immediate surroundings. Like an audible IV, it provided me a source of strength. Even if we aren't shells of ourselves with spiders on the brain, it's comforting to recognize those impulses in one another and know we aren't crazy, or if we are, at least we're not alone. With Morrison emoting on our behalf, we certainly are less so. There is a bridge back to humanity. As a listener, we can cast ourselves in any part we want: as the man himself, or the one being sung to.

Further healing power of the album rests in what is familiar. Because I was born in 1987, nineteen years after the songs were released, they've never not been there for me. They are literally familiar to my ear. My 2015 deep dive was not my first *Astral Weeks* experience. "Sweet Thing" appears on the 1990 compilation album *The Best of Van Morrison,* a staple of my childhood, on constant rotation during car pools and my parent's DJing dinnertime since its release. The reputation of *Astral Weeks* looms large over music lore and I heard the full album from time to time growing up. Thanks to streaming services later on, I always had access to my other favorite tracks from the record whenever I wanted them: "Astral Weeks," "Sweet Thing" "Cyprus Avenue," and "Madame George."

Regardless of your prior knowledge of *Astral Weeks*, the songs were crafted in nostalgia from their inception and are built to be familiar. This is not to say *Astral Weeks* sounds like any other album—on the contrary. This masterpiece is unique, timeless, from "another time, in another place." It is wholly its own. But the themes are familiar as memories: young love, reconciling where you are in your life and where you want to be, revising past haunts. The subjects are mystical and mythical, twinkling fairytales from childhood. Streets as proper nouns are name-checked. They could be your own streets, from your own past. "Sweet Thing" begins with the word "and" as if we too were part of that earlier, ongoing conversation. "And," as if it was a verse cast out from the Bible: the Gospel According to Van. Edging on reminiscent, but nothing formulaic.

Then of course there is the music itself. It speeds along, wheels in motions, rapid acoustic strums, the antonym of passive. "Madame George" has someplace to be. Summer is rushing in the loud, jazzy, "The Way Young Lovers Do." For further proof of the album's surprising speed, watch Glen Hansard cover "Astral Weeks," the aggression made possible by the source material. Or even better, get yourself a copy of the "Catacomb Tapes," Peter Wolf's 1968 bootleg recording of The Van Morrison Controversy playing in Boston before Van recorded the eventual studio album.

However urgently the songs' internal fire may burn, they are simultaneously gentle. They don't sleepwalk, but they tour dreamscapes and pastoral images, "way across the country where the hillside mountains glide." There's always an improvisational feel of the flute, kissing the tracks as delicate as powdered sugar raining over pastries. "Cyprus Avenue" sounds more like the embodiment of a dancing ballerina than "Ballerina," the [overdubbed] strings making your arms float up and down like a conductor's, or a falling of a leaf against the mild friction of air. The songs on *Astral Weeks* are what you need to hear when you want to jump into a winter harbor or curse out your boss. Without any of the triteness, it's a paced breathing exercise before we all had mindfulness apps on our phones to help us keep our cool. It's the album you could actually listen to at your dysfunctional office and complete your work and feel fulfilled.

For all the aforementioned pain described by mopey rock writers, myself included, this album is more about love than heartache. These aren't poppy love songs, with one-dimensional characters and easy, rhyming love in a predictable verse-chorus-verse pattern. *Astral Weeks*' love reflects a more authentic affection that ambles its individual path, where a character must vow to his beloved: if we can just be together, "I'll be satisfied/ Not to read in between the lines." Which, coincidently, may be a cheeky wink to listeners hung up on analyzing the lyrics. Bangs writes of "Astral Weeks":

> I haven't got the slightest idea what that "means," though on one
> level I'd like to approach it in a manner as indirect and
> evocative as the lyrics themselves. Because you're
> in trouble anyway when you sit yourself down to explicate just
> exactly what a mystical document, which is exactly what
> *Astral Weeks is, means.*

But of course words *do* have meaning. Bangs insists that Morrison's lyrics are "about a *person,* like all the best songs, all the greatest literature." And if literature bears analysis, and if, as Bangs does at the end of his essay, we can compare Morrison to a poet such as Federico García Lorca, then Morrison's songwriting can withstand close reading. A close reading and repeated playing.

The singer of "Astral Weeks" is trying to make peace with himself as he wrestles with his feelings of belonging, "I'm nothing but a stranger in this world/I got a home on high/In another land/So far away." He's doubting whether he can connect with anyone, "If I ventured…Could you find me?" Would his beloved, would his fans, would the world, follow him through this long and winding journey to craft his art, through "the slipstream/Between the viaducts of your dream?" He's "pushin' on the door" of artistic breakthrough "trying to do [his] very best" but his insecurities are made more intense due to imagined conversations with his own heroes, like Huddie Leadbetter. Who can't relate to that? That's how I still feel when I "talk" to Lead Belly. Or Bangs. And especially to Morrison.

Sources

Section Titles
The five section titles are culled from Van Morrison lyrics. "If I Ventured in the Slipstream" is a line from his song "Astral Weeks" appearing on his album *Astral Weeks*. "Turn Up Your Radio" is a line from his song "Caravan" appearing on his album *Moondance*. "Old Old Woodstock" is a line from his song "Old Old Woodstock" appearing on his album *Tupelo Honey*. "Looking for the Veedon Fleece" is a line from his song "You Don't Pull No Punches, But You Don't Push the River" appearing on his album *Veedon Fleece*. "Still for Searching for the Philosopher's Stone" is a line from his song "Philosopher's Stone" appearing on his album *Back on Top*, as well as a reference to Morrison's album *The Philospher's Stone*.

Liner Notes
The songs quoted in "Liner Notes" include John Prine's "Angel From Montgomery" appearing on his album *John Prine* and Morrison's "Sweet Thing" appearing on his album *Astral Weeks*.

The First Draft of *Astral Weeks,*
or The Emotional Labor of Janet "Planet" Rigsbee Morrison
The biographical material in "The First Draft of *Astral Weeks*, or The Emotional Labor of Janet "Planet" Rigsbee Morrison" is informed by Ryan H. Walsh's A*stral Weeks: a Secret History of 1968*. The poem references Morrison's "Ballerina," appearing on his album *Astral Weeks*. The song lyrics, "little angel child" culled from "Ballerina" are also used. (Walsh, Ryan H. *Astral Weeks: a Secret History of 1968*. Penguin Books, 2019.)

At the Langhorne Slim Show, East Side Milwaukee
The poem references the Langhorne Slim, whose given name is Sean Scolnick, and his song "Ocean City (For May, Jack, and Brother Jon)," appearing on his album *Lost At Last Vol.1*. where he also refers to Frank Sinatra.

Between the Viaducts of Your Dreams
The poem references Morrison's "Ballerina," appearing on his album *Astral Weeks*. The song lyrics, "between the viaducts of your dreams" are culled from the title track "Astral Weeks" from his album *Astral Weeks*.

folklore
The poem references Taylor Swift's album *folklore*, which features the song "exile," a duet with For *Emma, Forever Ago* musician Bon Iver.

Beside You
The poem references Morrison's song "Beside You," appearing on his album *Astral Weeks*. The song lyrics, "magic shroud," "you breathe in/you breathe out you breathe in you breathe out," and "pointed island breeze" are culled from "Beside You." The final line, "*Wheresoever she was, there was Eden—*" is a quote from Mark Twain's "Eve's Diary."

I Shall Watch the Ferryboats and They'll Get High
The song lyrics, "I shall watch the ferryboats and they'll get high" and "Jumping hedges" are culled from Morrison's song "Sweet Thing." "The Swimmer" refers to the short story by John Cheever.

For Bob, at Ben's Wedding
The poem references Jane Hirschfield's "Tree," reworking the line, "immensity taps at your life." The poem also references the Grateful Dead songs "Ripple," culling the lines "gold of sunshine," and "Friend of the Devil" which both appear on their album *American Beauty*." "Lisa Says" is a song by Lou Reed appearing on his album *Lou Reed*.

Sam Cooke is on the Radio and the Night is Filled With Space
The song lyrics, "Sam Cooke is on the radio and the night is filled with space" is culled from the Morrison song "Real Real Gone" appearing on his album *Enlightenment*. The poem references the song "Bring It On Home to Me" by Sam Cooke, covered by Levon and the Hawks (whose members later formed The Band) and Morrison himself.

Fret Noise
Greil Marcus is a rock critic, whose critical opinions expressed in this poem are informed by his book *When That Rough God Goes Riding: Listening to Van Morrison*. The poem references Morrison's albums *Astral Weeks, Veedon Fleece, No Guru, No Method, No Teacher, The Healing Game*, and *What's Wrong With this Picture?* The poem references Morrison's song "Linden Arden Stole the Highlights" appearing on his album *Veedon Fleece*, quoting the lines, "cleaved their heads off with a hatchet." Merry Clayton performs backing vocals on The Rolling Stone's song "Gimme Shelter" appearing on their album *Let it Bleed*. A patronus is a term from the *Harry Potter* fantasy novels written by J.K. Rowling. *Pottermore* is the official *Harry Potter* series fan website. Raymond Carver was a short story writer and poet. The poem loosely refers to Morrison's song "Fire in the Belly" appearing on his album *The Healing Game*.

Between the Viaducts of Your Dreams
The song lyrics, "between the viaducts of your dreams" are culled from the title track "Astral Weeks" from the album *Astral Weeks*. The poem refers to Morrison's song "Redwood" appearing on his album *Saint Dominic's Preview* and lyrics, "*It smells like rain,/ maybe even thunder*" are culled from the song as well.

And It Stoned Me, Prelude
The poem's title refers to Morrison's song "And It Stoned Me" appearing on his album *Moondance*. It also refers to The Velvet Underground album *White Light/ White Heat*. The song lyrics, "*if I knew Picasso*" are culled from "Mr. Jones" by the Counting Crows appearing on their album *August and Everything After*.

It Stoned Me Just Like Going Home
The poem's title refers to Morrison's song "And It Stoned Me" appearing on his album *Moondance*.

Caught One More Time Up on Cyprus Avenue
The poem refers to the Morrison song "Cyprus Avenue," culling a line for the title. It also refers to the song "Slim Slow Slider." Both songs appear on *Astral Weeks*.

Dweller on the Threshold
The title refers to the Morrison song "Dweller on the Threshold" appearing on his albums *Beautiful Vision*. "Dweller on the threshold" is a concept develop by the nineteeth-century theosophy writer Edward Bulwer-Lytton and developed further by Alice Bailey. "Bloodlife" is the title of a poem by Alyssa Morhardt-Goldstein published in *The Mackinac*.

The Last Time I was Drunk
The poem contains references to Grateful Dead songs, including "Shakedown Street" appearing on the album *Shakedown Street* and "Franklin's Tower" appearing on their album *Blues for Allah*. The mention of "The Mighty Quinn" in the poem is a reference to "Quinn the Eskimo (The Mighty Quinn)" a song by Bob Dylan first appearing on *The Basement Tapes*.

The Sweet Inspirations,
or In Defense of "Brown Eyed Girl"
The lines "*Sha la la la la?/* just like that" are culled from Morrison's song "Brown Eyed Girl" appearing on his album *Blowin' Your Mind*! In "Brown Eyed Girl" Morrison sings "down in The Hollow" which refers to a park in East Belfast where the Connswater River, nicknamed the Beechie through that stretch, flows. I refer to this in the lines, "Beechie/ that runs the whole length of The Hollow/ behind the row houses of Abetta Parade?"

While Walking Routinely to and From Work
The epigraph is from James Wright, "Lying in a Hammock at William Duffy's Farm in Pine Island, Minnesota." "The fields the fields are always wet with rain after a summer shower," is culled Van Morrison's "In the Garden" as performed on his live album *A Night in San Francisco*. Justin Vernon, known by his stage name, Bon Iver, sing "You're in Milwaukee, off your feet/And at once I knew I was not magnificent" in his 2011 song "Holocene," appearing on his album *Bon Iver*. Adam Duritz is the lead singer and principal songwriter for the band the Counting Crows. The indented lines are culled lyrics from their song, "Murder of One" appearing on their album *August and Everything After*. "Chain of Fools" is a song by Aretha Franklin appearing on her album *Lady Soul*.

Dwelling
The epigraph is from Morrison's song "Dweller on the Threshold" appearing on his albums *Beautiful Vision* and *Live at the Grand Opera House Belfast*. The song lyrics, "I've said I'm sorry by now at least once to just about everyone" are culled from the unreleased Counting Crows song "August and Everything After." The line, "This isn't it. This isn't it." is a reworking of a line, from the Lenea Grace's poem "Calgary, 1981" which appears in her debut poetry collection *A Generous Latitude*. The line, "let these delusions drown" is reworking the line, "let the great illusion drown" from Morrison's song "Dweller on the Threshold."

Warren Zevon Poems
The poem refers to the Warren Zevon songs "Werewolves of London" and "Accidentally Like a Martyr" appearing on his album *Excitable Boy*, culling the lines "after such a long, long time," from "Accidentally Like a Martyr."

Meditating to Madame George
The title refers to the Morrison song "Madame George" which appears on his album *Astral Weeks*.

On Being Pharrell but Probably Not Being Pharrell
Sgt. Pepper's Lonely Hearts Club Band is an album by The Beatles, produced by their longtime collaborator George Martin. This poem contains a quote from Libby Titus as printed in Levon Helm's autobiography, This *Wheels on Fire*, "they were all busy living up to the story of the Band and the whole Dylan myth." In this poem, the lines, "I don't wannabe Bob Dylan./ I want to be someone/ just a little more happy" is an alteration of the Counting Crows lyric, "I wanna be Bob Dylan./Mr. Jones wishes he was someone just a little more funky" from their song "Mr. Jones" appearing on their album *August and Everything After*. It also loosely refers to the Pharrell song "Happy" appearing on his album *Girl*.

Greenwich Mean Time
The lines, "My little girl I can't find/ She's five hours behind" are a quote from the Bell and Sebastian song "Chickfactor" appearing on their album *The Boy With The Arab Strap*. "5am Greenwich Mean Time" is a song by Morrison appearing on his album *The Prophet Speaks*.

Bill Remembers Watkins Glen
Salmons, Bill. Personal interview. 6 December 2019.

Wendy Remembers Watkins Glen
Summer Jam at Watkins Glen in 1973 was a rock festival that featured The Allman Brothers Band, of which Gregg Allman was a member. The lineup also included the Grateful Dead who performed their song "Sugaree." Ross, Wendy. Personal interview. 7 December 2019.

Stuart Remembers Van Morrison and Janis Joplin at the Cole Auditorium, University of Maryland, Friday, June 19, 1970
The line, "his tongue got tied," is a reference to the lyric in the Morrison song "Cyprus Avenue" where he sings "Yeah, my t-tongue gets tied/ Every, every, every time I try to speak." *Moondance* is an album by Morrison. The line, "It's too late to stop now" is a lyric first appearing in Morrison's song "Into the Mystic" from his album *Moondance*, but that phrase also acts as a mantra and is inserted into many songs in live performances. It is also the name of his

multi volume live album. The line "throw pennies" is a reference to displeased audience members that would throw pennies at Morrison during early stages of his career, as well as the lyric "Throwing pennies at the bridges down below" from his song "Madame George" appearing on his album *Astral Weeks*. Ross, Stuart. Personal interview. 7 December 2019.

Annotated Listening: "Live at the Grand Opera House Belfast"
The poem refers to the Morrison album *Live at the Grand Opera House Belfast*. Unless otherwise specified, all songs mentioned appear on that album. The lines "whispering shade of trees," his culled from Morrison's song "Full Force Gale." The italicized and indented lines, "*In the moss borne dark dank pools/ Rave on, down through the industrial revolution/Empiricism, atomic and nuclear age*" are a quote from the Morrison song "Rave on, John Donne." "Summertime in England" is a song by Morrison appearing on his album *Common One*. The line, "blowin' your mind!" refers to the Morrison album of the same name.

From Forest Hills Stadium, September 12, 2018
The poem refers to Morrison's song "Sweet Thing" appearing on his album *Astral Weeks*. The poem also references Jessica Hopper's book, *The First Collection of Criticism By a Living Female Rock Critic*.

What *Pet Sounds* Means to Me, or Franklin and I Go See Brian Wilson
Pet Sounds is a Beach Boys album, composed almost entirely by Brian Wilson. This poem contains the quote, "East coast girls are hip," a line from "California Girls" appearing on the album *Summer Days (And Summer Nights!!)*. This poem loosely refers to the Beach Boys song "Good Vibrations."

Dominique in Woodstock, NY, 1967
This poem contains a quote from Dominique Robertson as reported to Greil Marcus and published in hist book, *When That Rough God Goes Riding: Listening to Van Morrison*, "There's nothing here but dope, music, and beauty. If you're a woman, and you don't make music and you don't use dope, there's nothing here at all."

Imagining West Saugerties
Peter Max painted the cover art of The Band's album *Jericho*.

4% Pantomime
"4% Pantomime" is a song written by Morrison and The Band and appearing on The Band's album *Cahoots*. It refers to the 4% proof difference between Johnnie Walker Red and Johnnie Walker Black. The lines, "oh, Richard—" and "It was a gas, it was a smash" are culled from the song. The line, "old, old Woodstock" is culled from Morrison's song "Old Old Woodstock" appearing on the album *Tupelo Honey*. The line, "*well, I'm wasted and I can't find my way home*" is a culled from Blind Faith appearing on the album *Blind Faith*. Beak was a nickname for Richard Manuel, pianist for The Band, and Belfast Cowboy is a nickname for Morrison who perform a duet in "4% Pantomime."

Van at The Last Waltz
The line, "turning up" is culled from in the Morrison song "Caravan" appearing on the album *Moondance* and performed live with The Band at the Last Waltz concert. "Tura Lura Lural" also known as "Too-Ra-Loo-Ra-Loo-Ral (That's an Irish Lullaby)" is a song written in 1913 by composer James Royce Shannon. It was performed by Richard Manuel and Morrison at the Last Waltz concert. "Stagefright" is a reference to The Band song "Stage Fright" appearing on The Band album *Stage Fright*.

Morrison and Dylan Perform "Foreign Window"
The line, "singing about Rimbaud" is culled from Morrison's song "Foreign Window" appearing on his album *No Guru, No Method, No Teacher*.

A Mischief of Two
The line is culled from a traditional nursery rhyme "One for sorrow. Two for joy." The Counting Crows culled the same nursey rhyme for their song "A Murder of One" appearing on their album *August and Everything After*.

Looking for the Veedon Fleece
The poem makes references to Morrison's song, "You Don't Pull No Punches, but You Don't Push the River" appearing on his *Veedon Fleece* album. The following lines, are culled from that song, "Looking for the Veedon Fleece," "William Blake and the Eternals," "You don't push the river," and, "you don't pull no punches." This poem uses a quote from Seamus Heaney's poem "Postscript," which appears indented in italics.

The Streets of Arklow
"The Streets of Arklow" is a song by Morrison appearing on his album *Veedon Fleece*. The line in the poem, "*head be full/of poetry*" is an alteration of a line in the song "The Streets of Arklow."

Box of Rain
The poem's title takes its name from the Grateful Dead song "Box of Rain" from their album *American Beauty*, written by Robert Hunter and Phil Lesh.

Purple Heather
"Purple Heather" is an Irish folk song also known as "Wild Mountain Thyme" or "Will Ye Go, Lassie, Go?" Morrison covers "Purple Heather," appearing on his album *Hard Nose the Highway*. "When the Leaves Come Falling Down" and "Golden Autumn Day" are songs by Morrison appearing on his album *Back on Top*.

Northern Ireland Poetry
The epigraph is from Morrison's song "Got to Go Back" appearing on his album *No Guru, No Method, No Teacher*. The line "when *he* was a young boy back in Orangefield" is a reworking of a line culled from "Got to Go Back" as well. This poem refers to Gerald Dawe's collection of poetry, The Last Peacock. The line "coming down from Downpatrick" is culled from the Morrison song "Coney Island" appearing on his album *Avalon Sunset*. The line "RAVE ON!" is a reference to the Morrison song "Rave On, John Donne" appearing on his album *Inarticulate Speech of the Heart*. The line "Coney Island (baby)" is a reference to the actual island in County Down, the Morrison song, and the Lou Reed song and album *Coney Island Baby*.

Queens of the Slipstream
The poem refers to the Morrison song "Queen of the Slipstream," appearing on his album *Poetic Champions Compose*, as well as culling the line from the song, "far across the sea."

Ways of Looking at "Foreign Window"
The following lines are culled and/or reworked from the following poets and songwriters:
"Foreign Window," Van Morrison: "I was reading on the sofa, /I was singing every prayer."
"I spied her from the foreign window"

"I had gone down to Lake Geneva"
"If you get it right this time, / there's no need to revise."
"Keeping Things Whole," Mark Strand: "We all have reasons for moving."
"Other Ways," Trevor Hall: "Now I'm free to roam, everywhere I go/I feel like I'm home."
"August And Everything After," The Counting Crows: "I no longer know how to pray"
"The Drunken Boat," Arthur Rimbaud, Translated by Wallace Fowlie: "O, says Rimbaud, let me go into the sea!"
"Epitaph to a Dog," Lord Byron: "Oh man! says Byron, thou feeble tenant of an hour!"
"The Promise Land," Bruce Springsteen: "Driving all night chasing some mirage,"
"Promised Land," Chuck Berry: "tell the folks back home: /this is the promised land calling"
Traditional: "Make me down a pallet on the floor"
"Homeward Bound," Simon & Garfunkel: "where my thought's escaping,/ where my music's playing,"

And
The poem refers to two song from Morrison's *Moondance* album, "Glad Tidings" and "Everyone."

I heard Lead Belly and Blind Lemon on the Street where I was born
The poem's title is culled from the Morrison's song "Cleaning Windows" from *Beautiful Vision*.

Quantum Decoherence
The poem culls the lines "[doesn't] miss her" and "west down Ventura Boulevard" from Tom Petty's song "Free Fallin'" appearing on his album *Full Moon Fever*. The poem culls the lines "music of the spheres" from Morrison's song "Dweller on the Threshold" appearing on his albums *Beautiful Vision*. Goldstein, Bart. Personal interview. 23 March 2021.

The *Laughremen*
The epigraph comes from Bob Curran's *A Field Guide to Irish Fairies*. The line, "Why, must I always explain?" is quote from the Morrison song "Why Must I Always Explain?" appearing on his double album *Hymns to the Silence*.

Not Quite Stranded
This essay uses quotes from the following albums, books, and essays: Morrison's *Astral Weeks*, Lester Bang's "Astral Weeks," Jessica Hopper's *The First Collection of Criticism by a Living Female Rock Critic*, Greil Marcus's *When That Rough God Goes Riding: Listening to Van Morrison,* Herman Melville's *Moby Dick*, Van Morrison's *Astral Weeks*, and Ryan H. Walsh's *Astral Weeks: a Secret History of 1968.*

Acknowledgments

I am deeply grateful to the editors at the publications where the following work first appeared:

Aesthetica Magazine: "Quantum Decoherence"

Crazyhorse (now *swamp pink*): "folklore," "The First Draft of *Astral Weeks*, or The Emotional Labor of Janet "Planet" Rigsbee Morrison," and "Looking for the Veedon Fleece"

Phoebe Journal: "Not Quite Stranded"

Silver Needle Press: "For Bob, at Ben's Wedding" and "I Shall Watch the Ferryboats and They'll Get High"

Yemassee: "At Robert Johnson's Grave, Greenwood, MS"

Thank you to the entire team at Finishing Line Press for helping me realize this life-long dream. I am truly honored.

To me, poetry is a team sport. I am forever indebted to every creative writing workshop participant and facilitator whom I have been lucky enough to work alongside to hone my craft. The engaging contributions of my peers have helped shape me into the writer I am today. I am so appreciative of this community in general and especially of the following: Lenea Grace, Alyssa Morhardt-Goldstien, Su Cho, Peter Buzyński, the bar scene at Café Loup circa 2011, and my classmates at The New School and UWM.

Thank you to David Lehman, Craig Morgan Teicher, Mark Bibbins, Elaine Equi, Patrick Donnelly, Kimberly Blaeser, Liam Callanan, and Mauricio Kilwein Guevara for your wisdom. Thank you, Paul Maddern, for providing such a peaceful, nourishing respite at The River Mill, not to mention the County Down tour and additional Northern Irish history chats. Thank you, Storm Pilloff, for helping me across the big academic finish line.

Because it bears repeating, thank you to Lenea Grace for getting all my classic rock references and to Alyssa Morhardt-Goldstien for getting none of them. Your individual musical expertise and poetic chops were vital in checking and indulging my most esoteric impulses. You each showed care, humor, tact, and good taste when reading early drafts of my work and offering productive feedback. This book wouldn't exist without you and I would be far worse without your friendship.

Alyssa, I initially had the idea to annotate *Astral Weeks* for you and somehow it evolved into this collection. The themes I began to explore—female friendship, the relationship that we have with art, and have with one another through art—remain solidly on the page thanks in part to you.

Lenea, I've had no greater creative ally and have endless gratitude for your insight. I am so thankful for the bond we built over the years and even appreciate the discrepancies between our Spotify-most-played-lists. You've been an editing partner, collaborator, traveling companion, and cheerleader. There's nobody who gets my relationship with Van like you do.

Thank you to my "non-writing" friends and family who have supported my career, whether that was by asking about my art, letting me vent about rejections, attending a reading, or buying this book. Many of your names appear in poems in this book, but even when it doesn't, your support has sustained me more than you know.

I am so lucky that some of my closest readers are in my immediate family and even luckier that they are all rock historians in their own right. Thank you to my Mom, Betsy, for being the first person I ever analyzed lyrics with— "Cleaning Windows" at around eight years old. Thank you for telling me that yes, absolutely one could be happy cleaning windows, but that is best when coupled with artistic pursuits like "blowin' saxophone on the weekend in a down joint." Thank you to my Dad, Clarke, for raising us on every volume of Dick's Picks, all the Happy Bus tunes, for still listening and discussing every Andrew Hickey podcast. Thank you, Dad for the poetic pointers, even the ones I didn't take.

Thank you to my older sister Brett, the world's best copy editor, for so frequently being my second set of eyes and dyslexia defense. Thank you to my younger sister Kelsey for letting me send so many poems in a hurried rush and giving each their due. Thank you for gently giving it to me straight. You're a naturally gifted editor. I love you both so much!

Zach, my Sweet Thing, my muse, your love is instrumental in all that I do. Thank you, Love.

Thank you to Dalwhinnie, who has been at my side, under my desk, on my lap, laying on top of papers, on top of reference books, every step of the way as I wrote this. You heard these poems first, hearing them again and again, out loud, without judgment, through every tortured revision. You have let me cry into your fur when I've needed it, forced me out of my own neuroses and out for a walk, and kept me going like no other.

www.ingramcontent.com/pod-product-compliance
Lightning Source LLC
Chambersburg PA
CBHW030054170426
43197CB00010B/1518